Reed

Kids During the Great Depression

Lisa A. Wroble

The Rosen Publishing Group's
PowerKids Press™
New York

Published in 1999 by The Rosen Publishing Group, Inc.
29 East 21st Street, New York, NY 10010

First Edition

Book Design: Danielle Primiceri

Photo Credits: Cover, pp. 4, 8, 12, 15, 16, 20 © Corbis-Bettmann; pp. 7, 11, 19 © Archive Photos.

Wroble, Lisa A.
   Kids during the Great Depression / by Lisa A. Wroble.
      p.   cm.—(Kids throughout history)
   Includes index.
   Summary: Discusses the social and economic climate of the Great Depression as it related to the life and daily activities of children.
   ISBN 0-8239-5255-X
   1. United States—History—1933–1945—Juvenile literature. 2 United States—History—1919–1933—Juvenile literature. 3. Depressions—1929—United States—Juvenile literature. 4. Children—United States—Social life and customs—Juvenile literature. 5. United States—Economic conditions—1918–1945—Juvenile literature. 6. United States—Social conditions—1918–1932—Juvenile literature. 7. United States—Social conditions—1933–1945—Juvenile literature.   [1. United States—History—1933–1945. 2. United States—History—1919–1933. 3. Depressions—1929. 4. United States—Social life and customs. 5. United States—Economic conditions—1918–1945. 6. United States—Social conditions—1918–1932. 7. United States—Social conditions—1933–1945.] I. Title. II. Series: Wroble, Lisa A. Kids throughout history.
E806.W78 1998
973.91—dc21   97-44306
                                                                                                                  CIP
                                                                                                                  AC

Manufactured in the United States of America

Contents

UNEMPLOYED BUY APPLES 5c EACH

Troubled Times

The Great **Depression** (dee-PRESH-un) was a time in history from 1929 to 1941. After World War I, Europe was in **ruins** (ROO-enz). But business in the United States was booming. Because things were so good, America was able to lend money to many countries in Europe to help them build what had been destroyed during the war. America also traded goods with these countries. The price of goods rose throughout Europe and America. But American people and businesses still bought a lot of things, including **stocks** (STOKS).

◄ *Because they lost their jobs, many men had to sell apples on the street just to feed their families.*

Stock Market Crash

People can make money in the stock market by buying stock, or a piece of a company, and sharing in the **profits** (PROF-its). When profits go up, stock values go up. But in 1929, lots of people bought stocks on **credit** (KRED-it) and never paid for them. Many people owed money to businesses and banks for this stock. Profits went down. Stock values began to fall. Stock buyers were asked for the money they owed. But people were unable to pay. Soon stocks were worthless. The market had crashed. People, banks, and businesses lost a lot of money.

Crowds of confused people lined Wall Street on Black ▶
Tuesday, October 29, 1929, the worst day of the crash.

An American Family

Andy's father owned a store in New York City. After World War I, business was good. His father bought stocks and made enough money to expand his store. The family moved to a big house with plenty of rooms for Andy, his two brothers, and his three sisters. Times were happy—until the stock market crash. Then his father lost a lot of money. Andy's family struggled to keep the store open. But to save the store, they had to give up their house.

◀ *Many stores all across the United States were forced to close because of the stock market crash.*

Moving

Many families lost their homes during the depression. Some traveled west in hopes of finding work. The trip was often difficult. Sometimes families didn't know where they would stay each night. Many of these people made **shanties** (SHAN-teez) out of cardboard and scraps of wood.

Andy's family was lucky. They were able to move into an apartment building. However, much of the furniture they brought with them did not fit in their tiny apartment. Many things had to be thrown away.

To save money, many families were forced to move from big homes to tiny apartments. ▶

Food

Soup was a common food during the depression years. The small amount of meat and vegetables that Andy's family had would feed just a few of them. Andy's mother tried to stretch the family's food by making soup. They soaked up the soup with hard, crusty bread. This helped fill Andy's empty stomach. They ate plain oatmeal for breakfast. Milk and sugar had become a **luxury** (LUK-sher-ee). Andy's friend Frank often had to stand in long lines at the **mission** (MISH-un) just to get some watery soup and stale bread. His family didn't have any money at all.

◀ *Many people had no choice but to wait in soup lines for food.*

Clothing

Like food, clothing had to last. In better times, Andy had worn **knickers** (NIK-erz), socks that covered his knees, hard leather shoes, a shirt, a jacket, and a cap. Now, as he outgrew those clothes, he had to wear his brother's old clothes. These were patched and too big. Andy's sisters wore long dresses, shoes, and ankle-length socks. Tears and holes in their clothes were mended over and over. Old newspapers or cardboard were used to line the insides of shoes. This kept people's feet dry by covering the holes in the bottoms of their shoes.

14

Most children wore clothes that had been patched and sewn dozens of times. ▶

cat
little cat
See a little cat.
This
pretty
Oh see
Mother and
rabbits
His
A
ball
Pig

School

Though America was in **turmoil** (TER-moyl), school was still open. Andy and his brothers and sisters studied reading, writing, and arithmetic. Most boys and girls began school at the age of five. They studied until they finished at least the eighth grade, when they were twelve or thirteen. But during the depression, boys often dropped out of school to look for jobs or to beg for food and money. As time dragged on, fewer and fewer children could go to school. They simply had no clothes to wear.

◀ *Classrooms grew emptier as fewer children were able to attend school.*

Passing the Time

When Andy wasn't in school, he and his friends played in the streets. There weren't many cars to look out for because no one could afford them. Stickball, tag, and marbles helped kids pass the time. At home, Andy listened to the radio. Radio shows and songs like "Brother Can You Spare a Dime?" were well-liked. Movies, or picture shows, were also popular during the depression. Andy loved them, but they cost five cents! So he and Frank would often dream about going to the movies or even a New York Yankees game.

Because money was scarce, kids didn't have many toys and had to find different ways to have fun. ▶

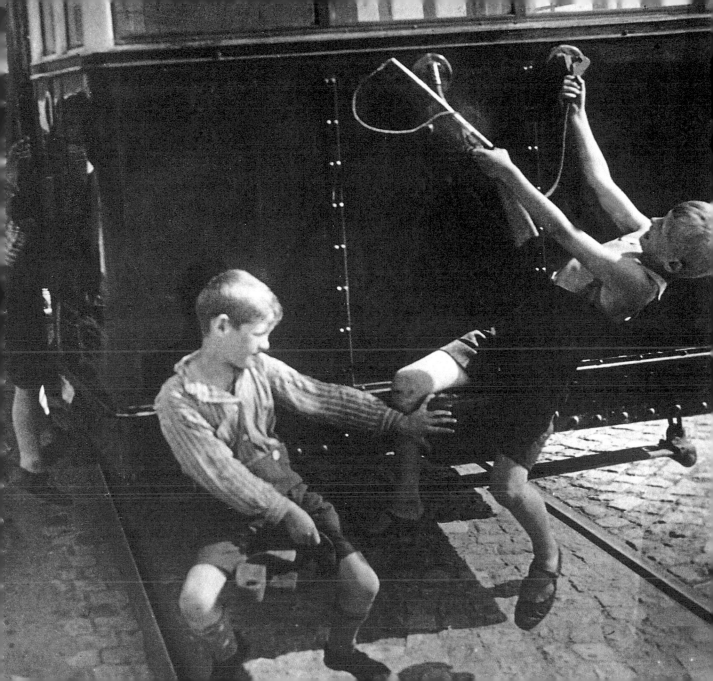

elping and oping

During the depression, 4 million people were without jobs. Andy's father gave food to Frank's family. People shared food with strangers too. But robberies became a big problem. And families were split apart when fathers and older boys left home and headed west to look for work. Then, in 1932, a man named Franklin Delano Roosevelt, or FDR, was elected president of the United States. FDR gave hope to the people of the United States. When he took office in 1933, he started to make changes right away.

◄ *FDR helped the United States so much that he was elected president four terms in a row.*

A New Deal

All of FDR's changes were part of a plan called the New Deal. **Relief** (ree-LEEF) was given to the poor. Jobs were created. Andy's brothers were hired to plant trees in national parks. Andy's father was able to hire new workers. People could finally afford to buy what they needed. But the depression did not really end until World War II began. Then, many people found jobs making things that helped American soldiers fight the war. Banks and businesses made changes to make sure that there would never be another depression.

Glossary

credit (KRED-it) When people buy something and promise to pay for it later.

depression (dee–PRESH-un) When banks and businesses lose money and it causes many people to lose their jobs.

knickers (NIK-erz) Short pants gathered at the knee.

luxury (LUK-sher-ee) Something that is nice or expensive but is not really needed.

mission (MISH-un) A religious center that helps people in a community.

profit (PROF-it) The money a company makes after all its bills are paid.

relief (ree-LEEF) Food, clothes, and money given by a government to help people in need.

ruins (ROO-enz) Something that is damaged so badly that it needs to be rebuilt.

shanty (SHAN-tee) A roughly built hut or shack.

stock (STOK) A piece or share of a company.

turmoil (TER-moyl) A time of trouble and confusion.

Index